Meditations

ON THE

Essence of Christianity

BY

R. LAIRD COLLIER, D.D.

BOSTON
ROBERTS BROTHERS
1876

Cambridge:
Press of John Wilson & Son.

Dedication

"Pain's furnace-heat within me quivers;
God's breath upon the flame doth blow;
And all my heart in anguish shivers
And trembles at the fiery glow:
And yet I whisper: '*As God will!*'
And in his hottest fire stand still.

He comes, and lays my heart all heated
On the hard anvil, minded so,
Into his own fair shape to beat it
With his great hammer, blow on blow:
And yet I whisper: '*As God will!*'
And at his heaviest blows hold still.

He takes my softened heart and beats it;
The sparks fly off at every blow;
He turns it o'er and o'er and heats it,
And lets it cool, and makes it glow:
And yet I whisper: '*As God will!*'
And in his mighty hand hold still.

Why should I murmur? for the sorrow
Thus only longer-lived would be;
Its end may come — and will to-morrow,
When God has done his work in me:
So I say trusting: '*As God will!*'
And, trusting to the end, hold still.

He kindles for my profit purely,
Affliction's glowing, fiery brand;
And all his heaviest blows are surely
Inflicted by a Father's hand:
So I say praising: '*As God will!*'
And hope in him and suffer still."

TO

Mary Price Collier

I DEDICATE this little book to Thee; not to thy Memory, but to thy Presence.

Whilst yet the Heavenly Glory was filling and flooding the chamber of death, and thy Spirit, quite upon the confines of the Eternal World, held the credential of prophecy, thou didst foretell my utter loneliness and dreariness without thy bodily presence, and didst promise that thy *Real Presence* should abide with me.

Thy dying words have been fulfilled. No day has come without the loneliness and the dreariness, but I have gone to duty when it has been oh, so hard, and oh, so dark, because of the assurance of thy Presence even in these hard and dark places.

We have had sweet communion upon the "things of the Spirit," and thou dost well know the thoughts, and art familiar with the sentences of these "Meditations."

Whatever in this book is untrue, or uncertain, or incomplete, is mine; whatever is true, or noble or helpful, is thine.

R. LAIRD COLLIER.

London, *February* 24, 1876.

CONTENTS

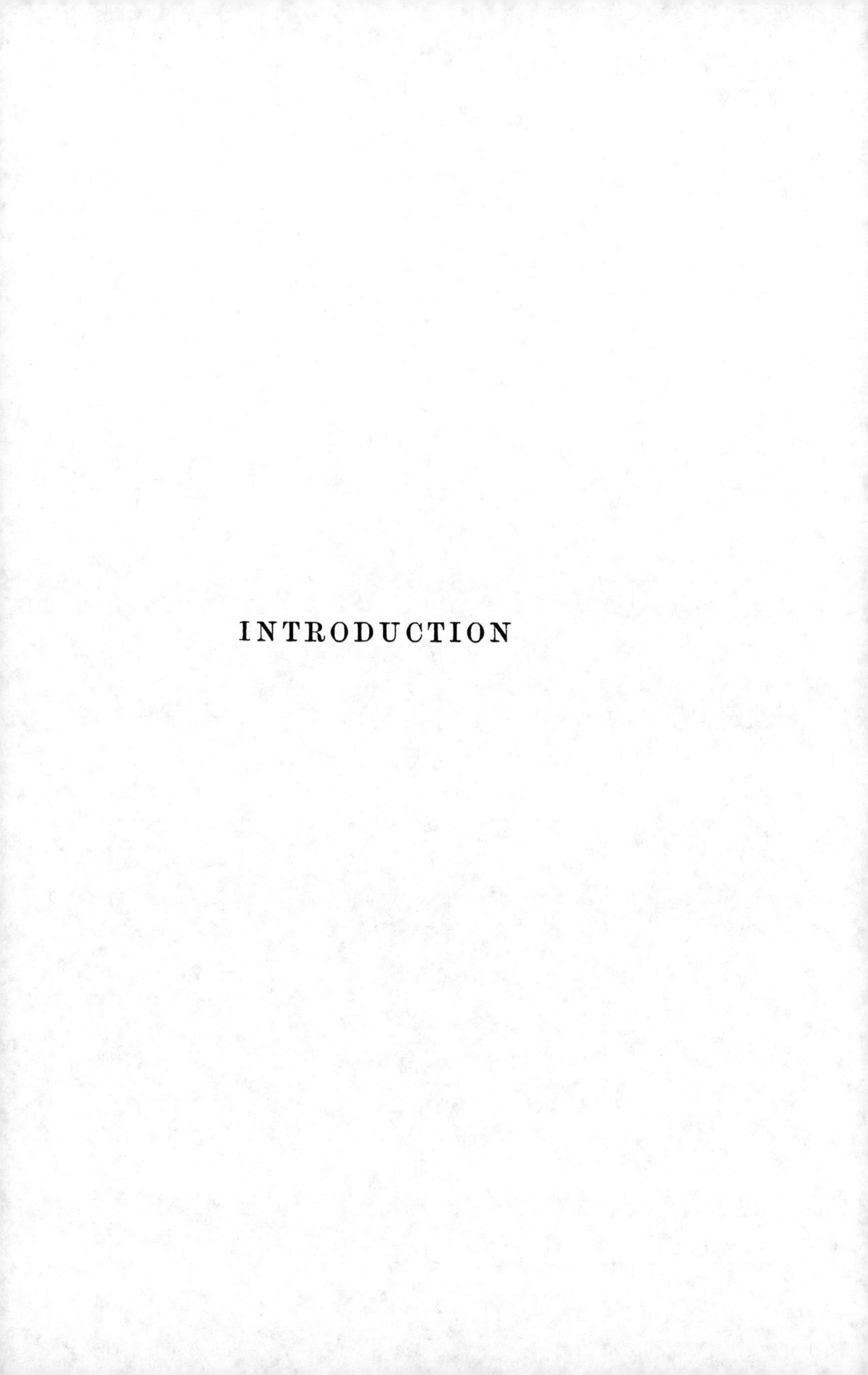

INTRODUCTION

"Teach how, yet, what here we know,
To the unknown leads the way,
As the light that, faint and low,
Prophesies consummate day;
How the little arc before us
Proves the perfect circle o'er us: —

How the marr'd unequal scheme
That on all sides here we meet,
Either is a lawless dream,
Or must somewhere be complete; —
Where or when, if near or distant,
Known but to the One Existent.

— He is. We meanwhile repair
From the noise of human things
To the fields of larger air,
To the shadow of his wings:
Listening for his message only
In the wild with Nature lonely."

AFTER reading Feuerbach's *Essence of Christianity*,[α] Büchner's *Force and Matter*,[β] and other books of like tendencies, I was led to look into my own heart to see if my faith in Christ and Christianity had been either destroyed or disturbed. I meant to make honest work of it. The *forms* in which I had held the "Old Faith" had in many cases been modified and in some wholly given up. But the "things essential," "the things which remain," became more real and more dear to me as I disencumbered them of their traditional and conventional

---

α. Das Wesen des Christenthums, von Ludwig Feuerbach. Leipzig, 1850.

β. Kraft und Stoff, von Ludwig Büchner. Leipzig, 1874.

phraseology, and consented to conform their outward expression with modern consciousness, and the original and permanent spirit of Christianity itself. Christianity is real; it has permanent contents; these are the most absolute ideas of spirit, life, duty, and aspiration, of which we know. Learning does not wage warfare on these sweet and sacred intuitions and sentiments of the soul, but it does, and must urge ceaseless and successful opposition to the superstitious and incredible forms in which they have frequently been held.

These "Meditations," then, grew out of my readings and inquiries, and were originally intended to meet, in some measure, many objections to Christianity, half formed if not wholly accepted, by serious and devout minds. However, I have deemed it best to shorten and simplify as much as I well could, these chapters, and thereby to seek for this little book a much wider reading and usefulness.

It does not assume, therefore, to be a critique upon such works as *The Essence of Christianity* and *Force and Matter*, although in many instances I use the thoughts and occasionally the language of these books, sometimes to show how they fall in with the truth of Christ, and sometimes to expose their fallacies and sophistries.

I have tried to find in my own heart the *reason* of my faith—to make it plain to myself that there was reality in religion, and enduring significance and saving grace in Christianity; and I here attempt to state the grounds of my faith rather as I feel them, than as I can put them into consecutive arguments. Logic, in its outward forms, is the vehicle of conviction and truth to comparatively few minds, whilst most are led to their deepest and enduring sentiments through their spiritual perceptions.

We cannot hold longer, against the *New Light*, the *Old Faith* in its old form. The Old Faith cannot perish, because it is real and true and good. But it will and must take its own form, and in the providence of God that form will be adequate, reasonable, and after the fashion of the times.

Heretofore, many have taken alarm when the perishable has perished and when the symbol has been proven to be superstitious, as though religion and worship would cease in the earth. But religion and worship have survived these changes in the outward dogmas and methods, and Christianity is more real and helpful by reason of the pulling down of these obstructions and the crumbling away of all authoritative and ecclesiastical interpretations.

Logic and reason must be met and satisfied. Christianity cannot survive—no form of religion can survive—which ignores their functions and claims. But religion is not based in these and does not make its first, certainly not its final appeal to them.

There is some knowledge greater than any speech, too subtle for any definitions. These "things of the spirit" we must "feel after" if haply we may find them.

If the spirit of man find God and can catch foregleams of immortality, this spirit will readily and sweetly make friends of reason and the logical understanding. Superstition has confused reason and confounded logic, and when these have found place and courage, they have entered vigorous protest.

Christianity is sufficient *to* itself. When its temporary and casual forms become an offence to fine sentiment and common sense, they must give way — die out. Leave it free, spiritually free, free as Christ himself was free, and each age and each civilization will give Christianity eyes and voice, hands and feet, as it shall please God.

I

THE ONLY GOD

"But neither passion nor sorrow I hear in this rhythmic steady course,
Only the movement resistless and strong of some all-pervading force;
The one universal life which moves the whole of the outward plan,
Which throbs in winds, and waters, and flowers, in insect, and bird, and man.

O, would that the unknown finer touch which makes us other than those,
Did not hold us so far asunder in soul, from their harmony and repose!
The self-same fountain doth life and growth to us and to them impart,
But only at moments we taste and know the peace which is Nature's heart.

And yet it may be that long, long hence, when aeons of effort have pass'd,
We shall come, not blindly impelled, but free, to the orbit of order at last,
And a finer peace shall be wrought out of pain than the stars in their courses know!—
Ah me! but my soul is in sorrow till then, and the feet of the years are slow!"

GOD is Spirit. This much we can say of God with great assurance of faith, only because we can say it through our spirits. Because our spirits affirm there is a God we believe in God. Not because there is a tradition of God; not for the reason that the Bible, and the catechism, and the Church have all taught God and about God; nor yet for the reason that it is conventional to believe in God; nor yet for the reason that, upon the whole, it gives us less anxiety of mind and less perplexity of logic to accept the doctrine of God, do we give our credence to it. But we believe in God because our spirits affirm Spirit. He offers some measure of insult to the integrity of his own spirit, who attempts to make the existence of God the subject of intellectual proof.

To try to prove some things is to demonstrate unbelief in them. My inquiry is in the interest of faith, so I have no formal arguments to offer to bolster up that which the only tendency of such arguments is to destroy.

When a man's spirit is crying out for the living God, to offer him a logical demonstration of God's existence, is like kindling a fire of straw to warm a man shivering in a Siberian frost.

The only logic of God is on this wise, — God is God; because we cannot prove him to be, we must acknowledge what we cannot deny, accept what we cannot refuse. Not to believe in some God is insanity, every sane man's soul refers itself to that which is eternal and infinite, as time and space are the symbols of something more real than time and space.

Disquisitions upon God are usually apologies for the God defined. Theodicy is a science by which glory is ascribed to a being who, brought into the plane of humanity, would be called unfair and cruel; that is, if any man should do what church theology says God has done and is doing, he would be justly called a human monster. Most sermons to which we have listened upon the goodness of God go to show that it is a great wonder that God is no worse, and that herein is ground for rejoicing, that, whilst God has made it probable — the most likely of all things — that most of the beings whom he has made and put into a disadvantageous set of circumstances will go into final and irrevocable perdition, it is a great mercy that there is any chance for the likeliest of us to escape it.

When a man is satiated he may not inquire whether there is food in the larder; when a child is content with his toys, he may not notice the presence or absence of his mother from the house. When a man is hungry, then he wants to know that there is "a haddock in the press," as the Scotch would say. When the child has notched his finger the bleeding frightens him, and he rushes to his mother.

Our hearts are not always on the watch for the coming and going of God, nor need our lips be like the dial in a gold-broker's room, telling the exact state of the spiritual market; but when we get very hungry, or our hearts get full of grief, so that we are clean undone, we cry out for our God. We may have been taught to call Him Jove or Jesus, or even Mary; still he or she is our only refuge in distress, the shadow of a great rock in a weary land.

I cannot hold controversy with an Atheist; he has me wholly at a disadvantage, he has the first affirmation that—"there is no God."

I cannot prove to him the second on my part, that there is. He can deride my superstition; I dare not sneer at him. The infidel can sneer, the believer would undo his faith by the same tactics.

When a man says he does not believe in God, I am sure he is either very fortunate or very unfortunate. He has never been hungry for God, never thirsted for living waters, never known the bleedings of a vicarious and grief-stricken soul, so he has been fortunate in this. Dare I say so? He counts it fortune. I say in reality, he has been most unfortunate — he has not yet breathed the breath of life.

The ocean sighs, it never sings: the winter winds, when they come, moan, never clap their hands in joy. All winds, too, come from heaven, so we cannot mistake the key to which its music is all set. Men will make glad music on a harp, but put it in one's window and let nature play upon its strings and the music is all minor, sombre, sad, sighing, wailing.

But this is the highest life. The multitude rejoice together, the saints dwell in solitary places. All nature is in the agony of redemption, — it is agony, — man redeems himself by agony; but there are bright clouds, and glory unspeakable, all about the grief of struggle.

So this man who says there is no God is a poor unfortunate brother, who has never felt the need of God; and, it is strange to say, these people are the product of civilization — the savages all have gods; the props of what we call civilization take the place now and then of God, only for a time however; they rot in the earth and the spirit falls, only to get upon surer foundation. God will claim the heart, and only comes when man has no other resource or help. So He magnifies himself into God. If one could dispose of Him like a problem of mathematics, or make a telescopic examination of Him, then He would not be God at all. He is God, because He is unsearchable, and His ways past finding out. God is not only a fact, but a light; not only a truth, but a life.

"Come in the glory of Thine excellence,
Rive the dense gloom with wedges of clear light,
And let the shimmer of Thy chariot wheels
Burn through the cracks of night — so slowly, Lord,
To lift myself to Thee with hands of toil,
Cl'mbing the slippery cliff of unheard prayer.
Lift up a hand among my idle days —
One beckoning finger, — I will cast aside
The clogs of earthly circumstance, and run
Up the broad highways where the countless worlds
Sit ripening in the summer of Thy love."

The history of the God-idea helps us but little towards a definition, for this is a history of gods. The gods of the peoples are as dissimilar as the races and nations themselves. Not only has each nation had its God, but each century, I may add, each individual. In tracing the development of this idea in the old scriptures of the world, we trace simply the dominant characteristics of the times and peoples themselves. As we approximate the beginning of history, and get back into the times when the aspect of nature was terrible, the being presumed to be the author of nature, or the master of nature, is terrible, — the awful, the sublime, and majestic.

When the habits of the people became pastoral and peaceful, God became a good shepherd; and when friendship became the bond of the social structure, and the home became a sanctity, God became a friend, a father, and a brother.

An exception must be made in the interest of history, which I cannot stop to make in the interest of dogmatism. Christianity, in its essence, unifies and fixes, as I believe, the one fundamental sentiment that makes God of any, and therefore so much, value to men — his imminence, only this makes God real at all; that he is not afar off, but here and now; not so much a creator of worlds as a re-creator of men; not *a* spirit, but *the* Spirit of all, in all, and through all. Language, when unperverted and left to tell its own story, tells the truth. The catechisms and theologic treatises result in the unity of conception, by what they call *attributes.* Men *attribute* certain things to God, and the highest of all these conceptions is God.

The most we know about God in a technical way is what the most god-like men have told us; and here we beg all claims to definition, in the use of the term "god-like," for if we disclaim all original idea of God, we cannot know what is like God. But the highest, purest, noblest ideal of being we call God, and the men who approach that in their lives, we call divine men. Then it is no great wonder that a superstitious age should have called such an exceptional symbol of that conception as Jesus was — God, and that a superstitious church should perpetuate the claim. There is no little human vanity in this; to see God and make God human is to make humanity God, and this is a great exaltation of men, for you and I are humanity.

The idea of humanity is incomplete without the idea of God; humanity refers itself to something to which it is responsible, and so has always worshipped — always will.

And to this end definite ideas have never been essential, because men have worshipped where ideas of God have not been the same. God lights up the prayer-book of the Jew and of the Christian, he escapes confusing phrases, and answers to the call of the needy heart. The primitive man of the primitive forests beats out a dolorous strain upon the rudest instrument—it is worship; the Christian gives up his spirit to the gorgeous ritualism of organ, trained musicians, incense, and ceremonial by priest and attendants — that is also worship. The thing essential is a hungry and thirsty soul. When we have put together unity, eternity, intelligence, beneficence, power, and imminence, we have affirmed of God the highest ideal that the most lucid and elevated spirits of the race have believed and felt. These qualities of being, when finite, constitute the highest man, when projected into the infinite, are God.

Then that worship which lifts man towards this ideal and brings him into communion, reverence, awe, and love, is the one best helpfulness. To break away from this is death and despair, before it becomes death and hell. To breathe this air of worship is to turn the spirit of the sick to the open window where perfumes and invigoration are wafted in.

Then I conclude that only that doubt damns which has in it no element of devoutness and aspiration. When a man says in his intellect "There is no God," I still trust his heart will batter away at his intellect day and night, until the heart makes the intellect see visions, — for really there is a higher nature in every man which enfolds the intellect, and takes it captive. There comes a time, I trust, in every man's life, when no intervention of cold speculation can shut out the need of God from the heart; and if it occur that man in the dreary winter days is a pessimist, we will believe that when the first spring days come back he will be an optimist, the doubt will succumb to faith, and this highest and truest nature will affirm there is a God, who will answer the man that cries unto Him: there is no deaf heaven, and no vain prayer. The hearing God will answer "not always according to the haste of the praying child, but surely according to the calm course of His own infinite law of love."

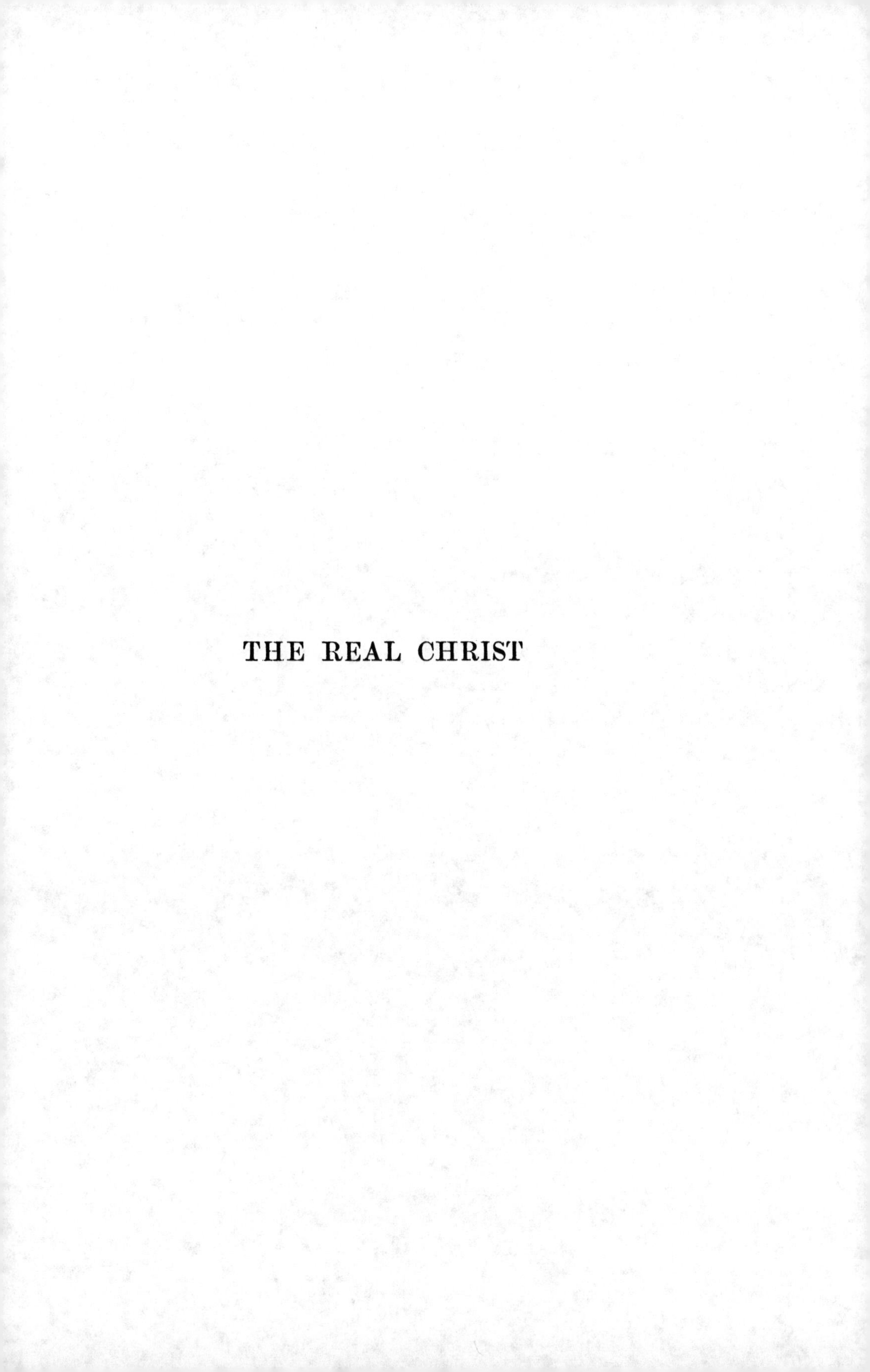

THE REAL CHRIST

Like a cradle rocking, rocking,
  Silent, peaceful, to and fro,
Like a mother's sweet looks dropping
  On the little face below,
Hangs the green earth, swinging, turning,
  Jarless, noiseless, safe and slow;
Falls the light of God's face bending
  Down and watching us below.

And as feeble babes that suffer,
  Toss and cry, and will not rest,
Are the ones the tender mother
  Holds the closest, loves the best, —
So when we are weak and wretched,
  By our sins weighed down, distressed,
Then it is that God's great patience
  Holds us closest, loves us best.

O great heart of God! whose loving
  Cannot hindered be nor crossed;
Will not weary, will not even
  In our death itself be lost —
Love divine! of such great loving,
  Only mothers know the cost —
Cost of love, which all love passing,
  Gave a Son to save the lost.

Saxe Holm.

I HAVE little hope of disposing any mind to greater faith *in* Christ: indeed, this is not my aim. The wavelets of rose odours are not fit subject for intellectual speculation and discussion. The philosophy of one's love for one's mother, or the magic power of a memento, cannot very well be defined: to attempt definition is to unsanctify; here assertion is vulgarity, sometimes hypocrisy.

Then, if my words seem without logical connection, I beg to attribute this to the subject I treat, and ask to be followed — not so much in thought as in heart — from the verbal form to the spiritual import, where I promise some degree of sequence.

I have a strong persuasion that I may be led to

say somewhat to strengthen faith in the faith *of* Christ. To have faith *in* Christ is something, though very little: to have the faith *of* Christ is every thing, — this is to have heaven and God.

Here is a life whose passion was truth, whose pleasure was purity, whose product was peace. We partake of these holy delights in some measure when we partake of the faith *of* his life. Christ had great faculty for leading men to these, — to religion, to God, and so was a mediator between man and God. Not a mediator between man and himself, for he came not to show us himself, but to show us the Father. So faith *in* God is the faith *of* Christ; the very mission of the Master is hindered and defeated when faith stands still *in* him. This is obstruction, not mediation. If this spiritual instrument stops the vision by the murkiness of its own lenses, this obscurity is simply the dust that ages of false and scholastic speculation have accumulated. This brushed away, and the spiritual eye is unhindered, ay, helped to see that which, without it, it could see not at all, or at least as afar off, minified, a speck clothed in haziness. There is a sense in which, therefore, faith *in* Christ hinders and annuls the faith *of* Christ.

The view which makes of the Christ a substitute is therefore only a false and vicious view, whether it regards the action of his life in either direction toward man or God. He is a substitute for neither; he is a mediator of both.

The eye of the Deity needs no medium, his heart none. There is in the loving Father no antithetical disposition toward his children. He was as near to Adam as to à Kempis, only à Kempis knew his nearness as Adam could not. The Christ became a mediator of the knowledge, not of the fact.

One form of Christian speculation has made the sufferings of Christ have reference to God. That in some way Christ made it possible for God to relieve Himself of a moral difficulty; that Christ made it possible for God to be just in Himself, and merciful toward His children. We, on our part, cannot see in this speculation any element of reality; to us, it is false and harmful, — false to theodicy, and harmful to morality. It calls something justice in God which we should call injustice in man. Then this speculation is wholly a needless one. If the sufferings of Christ in any wise modified either the disposition or enactment of God, this is not our part or share in the matter.

We know that the holy life of Christ, its absolute purity and beauty, the holy death of Christ, the seeds of which were planted in the voluntariness with which he took upon his heart the suffering and sin of the whole world, are an atonement; they bring a moral power into the world — a new kind of power — a new current of life which moves men to pity and mercy.

The *real* Christ is the law of the conscience made flesh; this law is the ideal God, and His will; then "God manifest in the flesh" is Christ.

Whether any human being in actuality ever realized this law in himself has no essential relevancy to our discussion; the effort to get rid of this conjecture and belief imposes a tedious mental and greater moral task upon him who attempts it.

It is much easier to accept Christ as the demonstration of God, than to deny it: this latter brings great perplexity in every way, for the universal Christian consciousness has invested Christ with this ideal, if in himself he is not such; and so far criticism has made sad work of separating between the intrinsic and extraneous reality, — both are real.

Christianity has succeeded in giving to its votaries a visible, living, personal law, in the Christ of its Gospels. If in himself he was not this realization, the Christian thought has invested him with it. There is in humanity a need of this personification of the law of the conscience. Plato, the intellectual Messiah, said of God, "I have sought Him, but He cannot be found; though every ray of the sun became my torch, darkness has fallen around me."

Christ, the spiritual Messiah, said, "Blessed are the pure in heart, for they shall see God."

This ideal in Christ is not less lofty after all these centuries of partial appreciation and following. Just as the Christian world moves up in the scale towards human perfection, this ideal Christ moves up in the scale of being. If, then, men have invested Christ with a quality of divinity which, in fact, he did not possess, we probably shall never know where to draw the line between that with which God endowed him, and that with which loving disciples have invested him.

There is a beautiful and spiritual sense, if withal somewhat mystical, in which the mediative Christ is a God manifested as man, and a man manifested as God.

Any abstract truth is difficult of comprehension: symbols and figures of speech frequently make the illustration of a truth plain, which otherwise would be obscure or unthinkable; we know what life is, because we know what a man is, or a flower is. When the abstract word "life" is used, we know what is meant, because we think of life in man, or life in a flower, or the life of something; we think of eye or limb in activity, we think of root or branch.

God is spirit or God is life; we think of spirit and life as active in Christ. So in this way Christ is God, known personally.

We may know a person by hearsay, or we may know an author by his writings; but if he be such an one as we long to know, there is an unfilled and aching void until we have seen him face to face, until we have known him personally.

"And the Word was made flesh, and dwelt among us, and we beheld his glory, the glory as of the only-begotten of the Father full of grace and truth."

The Word has been spoken. Christ is God speaking or personally communicating himself to man. Christ is the blessed certainty that God is what we wish Him to be. Indeed, I am ready to say that the idea of a personal God, dissociated from the idea of a corporeal God, is unthinkable. History confirms this view. Only those religions which hold to the possibility of the divine incarnation hold to the belief of the divine personality. Christ is God made flesh; that is, Christ is God become a person.

God, to be of any conscious helpfulness to man, must have a human expression; that is, to sympathize with suffering, must be the subject of it. So it is beautifully said of Christ: "He is touched with a feeling of our infirmity." "He also suffered being tempted, wherefore he is able to succour them that are tempted."

It is not only superficial but very mistaken to say that Christianity reveals three divine personalities. It is exactly the meaning of Christianity to deny this, and to illustrate that there is one personal God, revealed in the one man Jesus, who *so* is the real Christ.

The Holy Ghost is a term of purely arbitrary use in the Scriptures, as the gift of the Father, or of the Son, or of both, but usually signifying simply the Spirit of God.

The Olympian gods fulfilled the wants of the imagination by the element of splendour. Christianity fulfils the wants of the heart by the element of sympathy. The life of Jove was that of the mighty; the life of Jesus was that of the lowly.

The love of any thing noble and beautiful is the gate to heaven. So a child, a woman, a man, may be in some sense a mediator. To love Christ — in himself child, woman, and man — is to dispart the clouds, and let us into the inner glory. Only think of the dreariness of that child's soul who said he had no recollection of ever having been kissed. This spirit through which had swept only the chilling winds of the world's neglect could have no sense of heaven's love and watchfulness. What a revelation the life of Christ is to such an one! Where such an one loves Christ what a divine transfiguration!

If, now, I should pass away from these, to me, most holy and delightful reflections to formal definitions and dogmas, it would only be to repeat the sorry way the world has had of substituting stubble for the food of angels. It would be to give up certainty for uncertainty, knowledge for ignorance, faith for doubt.

I know nothing of Christ's pre-existence, or his eternal sonship. I cannot understand any trinity in God, or any need in God of appeasing Himself, or satisfying any demands of His law. I shrink from these poor frightful unrealities, as one who having known the communion of angels, would shrink from the fellowship of demons. I know nothing whatever of the supernatural. We find Christ just where our devotion and our faith should consent to leave him, in the plane of nature and humanity.

I cannot understand any thing about his miraculous birth, or his miraculous death; it is enough for me to hold the beautiful thought, that he was begotten of God, and that when he had fulfilled his days, he went home to his Father. To express this elevated conception, his loving biographers have thrown strange language about it, and so clothed it in purity and glory, that some have lost sight of the spiritual thought in the poetical imagery.

Though his mother was never so chaste and holy, her dear son never dishonoured her. She gave him a body; but his spiritual features were those of his Father. He came into the world not to show us his mother, but God.

He is, so far as we know, the finest flower of humanity; its son — its best son, and its best beloved son. Best and best beloved because so much like his Father; so much like Him that we know of no other son of whom we can say, "he is just like his Father, the very image of Him, he reminds us of his Father." Yes, this is the one wonderful fact about Jesus, he *reminds* the world of God. To manifest God, the spirit of God must be in him.

The Father's life has gone out into the life of His son, as blood passes from father to son, to give its own quality of temperament and physique. So Christ does something more than manifest God — he *demonstrates* God.

The real Christ may not answer exactly to the portraiture as painted severally by the four inspired artists of the Gospels. They did so well, that the debt of gratitude which we owe them we can never pay. Especially the loving John, who caught a glimpse of his Master's inner life and glory, and so reflected it that the strength of his colours have lost nothing with age.

The image of the Christ we have is so like God, and yet so like man, it serves well the divine and needful purpose of mediator between the two. Indeed, we never knew how very alike human and divine nature were, until the race saw Christ; so that having seen him we dare conclude that nature itself is a unit, — not two, but one; one in Christ Jesus. He fulfils the idea of both. We have no higher idea of man than Christ is, and no higher idea of God than Christ has revealed. He was the revelation himself, finitely: the essence of this is in him, the expanse of this is God.

Indeed, Christ seemed "empty of all save God." He was of God, according to his measure, which, nevertheless, had the limitations of humanity and finiteness. He was all that a perfect man could be. In his perfection he was like God, in his limitation he was like man.

The world has never been left without mediums and mediators of approach to God. The highest spirits of the East have got very near to the heart of God, by getting very near to the hearts of their own prophets. Those who have stood close to Buddha have stood close to God. Himself high up in the heavens, he has lifted many to his side, and to God's.

But his image has fallen upon the world obliquely. He gives light to a nation. Rising in the East, this sun stands still. Christ is the light of the world. Rising in the East, this sun has girdled the earth, and lighted up all zones with its own splendours. As the world has not yet conceived a more perfect pattern, it has not asked for one, and will not whilst it remains true as now that man knows no holy desire unsatisfied, no spiritual want unmet, no immortal aspiration unfulfilled in Christ our Lord.

THE KNOWN SPIRIT

Good tidings every day,
God's messengers ride fast,
We do not hear one half they say,
There is such noise on the highway,
Where we must wait while they ride past.

Their banners blaze and shine
With Jesus Christ's dear name,
And story, how by God's design
He saves us, in His love divine,
And lifts us from our sin and shame.

Their music fills the air,
Their songs sing all of Heaven;
Their ringing trumpet peals declare
What crowns to souls who fight and dare,
And win, shall presently be given.

Their hands throw treasures round
Among the multitude.
No pause, no choice, no count, no bound,
No questioning how men are found,
If they be evil or be good.

But all the banners bear
Some words we cannot read ;
And mystic echoes in the air,
Which borrow from the songs no share,
In sweetness all the songs exceed.

And of the multitude,
No man but in his hand
Holds some great gift misunderstood,
Some treasure, for whose use or good
His ignorance sees no demand.

These are the tokens lent
By immortality;
Birth-marks of our divine descent,
Sureties of ultimate intent,
God's Gospel of Eternity.

Good tidings every day,
The messengers ride fast;
Thanks be to God for all they say;
There is such noise on the highway,
Let us keep still while they ride past.

Saxe Holm.

THERE is some one holy thing between the heart of every man and God — the death of a mother, or the birth of a child, or some experience more occult than either of these, that serves as a point of confluence between the infinite Spirit and the finite spirit. This fact, whatever it may be, is the Secret Place of the Most High, and the Holy of Holies for the human spirit. It is that point in the life of each when life itself ceases to flow in, and begins to ebb out, — that is, when life is no longer sacred to the individual for the purposes of the individual, but sacred for the universal life of the world. In Jesus Christ this point was just that at which he became the medium of contact between God and man expressed in the phrase, "I in them, and Thou in me."

That which is intellectually unknown *in* God, is intellectually unknown to man. The Spirit of God witnesses to the spirit of man, and it is the most singular felicity in the relation of the infinite Spirit to men, that He never leaves Himself without this witness. The consciousness of it is seldom continuous. It is compared to the wind which comes and goes, we cannot always tell whence or whither. We hear its music, as of the "still small voice," as it touches sweetly the chords of life, deepest life, in us, and then passes on its way. The memory of its music it consents to leave with us, and this is the blessed surety and earnest of the Spirit.

I have already said this has some association in the life of every man, and I cannot believe that there can be an exception to this custom of the Spirit's operation. Man having come out from God, seeks to go back to God: had he been born of material nature, the grave would satisfy all his aspirations, he would be content to go to that from which he came; and when the mother earth threw around him her secure and strong arms, this couch would be the final peace and rest. Indeed man would know of nothing, and dream of nothing higher than his own origin: born of earth, being of the quality of the earth, he would be of the earth, earthy. But no man has been wholly left without the *reminiscence* of his original nature, so his heart and his flesh cry out for the living God.

The world itself, and its treatment of him, may seldom give hints of his origin, but now and then he will meet a man and receive a kindness which will remind him of God.

The Spirit of God works greatly and incessantly until it finds a lodgement in each heart — some soil is fertile, and some is sterile. The fruit of the Spirit is early seen in some lives, and will ultimately be seen in all lives. "The latest fruit will ripen at last."

The man may not always know when he enters this "whispering gallery" of the Spirit, and just at what point he first stood within this "holy of holies." He knows a new element has entered into his life, when or how he cannot determine sometimes even for himself — there are some things so solemnly sacred, that they cannot be made matter of even mental record. Indeed, the Spirit will not tarry for the slow movements of chronology. With God a thousand years are but as one day, and sometimes one day is as a thousand years; it is the nature of the thing that gives it significance, not the time required in doing it. Time is like space; there is so much of it, that for only a little section can we find names, such as day, week, month, year, century, and so on; as we say earth, moon, sun; and when we get through our list, already so long for the memory, the rest is nameless.

Few men *abandon* themselves to this call of the Spirit, but most men know of it; I do not mean to say that there are not some who are so open-eyed and free-hearted that they know the exact instant when this angel enters in, and when it folds its wings in peace and gives rest.

It is usually the way of the Spirit to make his presence felt most when it is most needed. When the children of integrity were in the fiery furnace, the form of the Fourth was seen. This was just when they needed God; it was their extremity.

It is a psychical fact, physicians tell us, that it is the rarest thing to find a patient afraid of death when just at its door. When one gets so far out of this world as to catch glimpses of the other, that other is revealed as very beautiful and full of welcomes.

The last impress which the spirit gives to the flesh is very lovely. We often remark a spiritual expression, — an expression of peace and tranquillity, — upon the face of a corpse which the subject of it seldom wore in life.

God is very good to permit the spirit to see what He has in reserve for it, and then to give it time to write this upon the face of death, so that the memory of death is pleasant, when the fear of it is gone.

When man is sufficient of himself, then he cannot believe his sufficiency is of God; when man is a god to himself, he wants no other, that is, he *feels* the *need* of no other. But when a great grief comes to him, he cannot see through it, or his way out of it, until God's Spirit so fills it, that it becomes translucent, and then a great grief is an ineffable peace.

There are some souls so sensitive and responsive to the spiritual, that whilst the memory of a lost friend is very vivid and precious to them, they are conscious of the presence of the same influence which this friend exerted over them before death. This is the soul of that which has been universal in the most mystical phases of religion—prayer *for* the dead, and prayer *to* the dead. And this defeats the philosophy of modern spiritualism, which interposes the voice of a stranger between the communion of two loving and affianced souls. This *spiritualism* is the most unspiritual of all conceivable things—so hard, so cold, so chilling, that it usually ultimates in the denial of Spirit, or atheism.

It is the way of the Spirit further never to give pain to the pain-bearer. The pain may *actually* remain, but the peace superinduced relieves from the sense of it.

Rubens understood this divine philosophy when he painted the crucifixion of St. Peter. The apostle is nailed to a cross, head downward, attitude and torture doing all they can to bring out the physical suffering and agony of the holy man in every limb and feature; and yet there is this infilling peace, this expression of triumph, and "the glory which excelleth," surmounting the whole man, and so dominating the suffering and agony that it does seem the cross cannot longer fix him to earth, he must be off to God.

The instant the *Son of man* came to man in the furnace the fire lost its power—its very quality of burning was gone.

And how little we know of the joys of suffering! Sometimes we think that people find pleasure, as we say, in being miserable. There are persons so situated in life that there is nothing in their outward circumstances to suggest unhappiness, and yet these persons are not happy; they know the Spirit teaches them it will not do to be happy *in* the outward conditions; so they are usually the most miserable, for they have not found out how to be happy *in* God. The knowledge of the Spirit, then, comes not by intellection, but by revelation. This I have already striven to make plain, not by the words of argument, but by the phrases of spiritual suggestion.

When the man has had the revelation, he has the knowledge, so that there is no Spirit but the *Known Spirit.*

The Spirit, as a distinction in the Godhead — something having official relations with us, in virtue of the official relations of the Son — is a figure of speech — in fact, a figment. There is no such thing, and if there were, we could know nothing of it. We can only know the Spirit as the subjective activity of God. We can know nothing of that polytheism of which the Spirit is one of the Gods. Such a Spirit is a phantom. Such a conception demands that a man should think the opposite of what he can think — that is, that he should think a phantom a reality.

The most plausible way of stating the doctrine

of the Trinity is this: "God is a personal being, consisting of three persons." And this statement in its last analysis is this: Three are one: the plural is singular. This is not thinkable; no intellect can comprehend this — only superstition can accept it. When the superstitious mind holds this at all, it is — it must be — with such subjective modifications as make it capable of believing it, which is equal to not holding it at all.

I conclude, then, that the Known Spirit is not "God the Spirit," of Church theology, but the Spirit-God of Christian consciousness. And the knowledge of this Spirit no man is left wholly without, for Spirit answers to spirit. There is no knowledge so real as this: what the spirit of man perceives of the Spirit of God, that a man knows as he knows nothing else. This is not the *rock* of certitude, but the very *ground* in which the rock itself finds foundation for the whole superstructure of the religious life.

The man who professes not to believe in the Spirit ought not to profess to believe in morality itself, for morality is nothing other than the Spirit speaking. Moral distinctions are the distinctions which the Spirit defines. The Spirit says what is right and what is wrong — what we ought and what we ought not to do. The universal conscience of man is the Spirit of God; or rather, conversely stated, the Spirit of God is the universal conscience of man. In this the religious Quietists have always held the substance of truth; if duty is to be discovered by any process, it is by heeding the inner voice; familiarity with the tones and speech of the Spirit is the essence of religion.

This essence of religion each man must know for himself; the fruits of it we can see in each other, like autumn days, whose tints we can describe, whose spirit we cannot define.

The Spirit of God, *in reality*, dwells everywhere. This can be known, however, only under certain conditions. We must bring peace, resignation, acquiescence, purity to God — all the products of the Spirit — if we would have the communion and fellowship of the Spirit.

In other words, the soul must be responsive to the voice of God, willing and wanting to hear, and to heed its words, before we can feel that we are the friends of God. "The Spirit itself must bear witness with our spirit that we are the children of God."

These terms, "communion" and "fellowship," are the singularly felicitous phrases by which the soul's recognition of God and God's recognition of the soul are set forth.

Precious words! They stand illumined and full of illumination, telling of the child's privilege in the presence of his Father.

We cannot see this communion and fellowship, but they give us eyes to see even "the excellent glory of God." He who knows this, then, can see the footprints of the Deity, not only where His gracious prodigality has flooded loftier natures with genius and faculty, but in the most barren and waste places of humanity; even here eyes are opened to see heaven upon the very confines of hell.

There is one especial direction where it is always

profitable to meditate upon the fruit of the Spirit. We are very accustomed to the sounds of the world's conflicts, and this is the more strange when we remember the concords of God's own universe — how sweetly the machinery of the universe works, and this because it works with God, for God, and in God. The world we inhabit moves on its axis and round its centre as quietly, as peacefully, as a new-born infant sleeps; and God holds it in his heart, just as the mother does her child. But the world that inhabits us — how full of discordances and inharmonies! Nations war for classification as first or second or third-rate powers, or for this or that enlargement of boundaries by this or that acquisition of territory. Sects of religion are not forges, wherein the spirits of men are welded in love together, but ràther arsenals, where weapons of warfare are in process of making — weapons of words — cold, deathful words of theologic creeds, which divide brothers into armies, not to fight all enemies of humanity, but each other. It is sacrilege — oh! so heinous — when this warfare is carried on in the name of that Spirit whose fruit is peace. The Spirit leads to unities, not divergences. It gathers, not to scatter abroad. It gives liberty to think; for "where the Spirit of the Lord is, there is liberty." But of this sense of liberty is born peace. There is, too, a higher, truer peace of the Spirit than mere outward agreement; it is the repose of the spirit of man in the Spirit of God — the very peace Jesus had, and which, without assumption or the seeming of it, he had to give to men. The peace of God, which passeth all understanding, was the peace the Master gave to his disciples — *gives* to his disciples.

And what though it pass the understanding of it! What though the intellect is ever lagging behind the realization, and only catches glimpses of partial outlines fading away in the infinite! To unfold the highest mystery of life to the spirit of man, Jesus justified faith in it by suffering and pain, and by the beauty of his life, born of the suffering, and the pain, and the mystery.

> "One heart beats in all nature, differing,
> But in the work it works; its doubts and clamors
> Are but the waste and brunt of instruments,
> Wherewith a work is done."

The Spirit that cradles the universe in its heart, and whose smiles, as over an infant, are the streaming tints of purple and azure and gold which play over the features of the heavens as the sun goes to rest, will hold us as dearly while we live, speak to us when we ask, and, when our mortal lips can no longer ask, will give us in death infinitely more than we could think in life.

IV

THE RIGHT RELIGION

Like a blind spinner, in the sun
I tread my days;
I know that all the threads will run
Appointed ways;
I know each day will bring its task,
And, being blind, no more I ask.

I do not know the use or name
Of that I spin;
I only know that some one came
And laid within
My hand the thread, and said, "Since you
Are blind, but one thing you can do."

Sometimes the threads, so rough and fast
And tangled, fly;
I know wild storms are sweeping past,
And fear that I
Shall fall; but dare not try to find
A safer place, since I am blind.

I know not why, but I am sure
That tint and place,
In some great fabric to endure
Past time and race,
My threads will have; so from the first,
Though blind, I never felt accursed.

I think perhaps this trust hath sprung
        From one short word
Said over me when I was young, —
        So young I heard
It, knowing not that God's name signed
My brow and sealed me his though blind.

But whether this be seal or sign
        Within, without,
It matters not; the Lord divine
        I never doubt.
I know he set me here, and still,
And glad, and blind, I wait his will.

But listen, listen, day by day,
        To hear their tread
Who bear the finished web away,
        And cut the thread,
And bring God's message in the sun,
"Thou poor, blind spinner, work is done."

H. H.

RELIGION is essentially one, and in its substance cannot be two or three, any more than light can be two or three, or truth can be two or three; the light may be modified by its mediums, "for there is one glory of the sun, and another glory of the moon, and another glory of the stars; for one star differeth from another star in glory:" but withal, the light is one.

The prism reveals the elements of light, its constituents of colour, or light seen in its separations; but light is one: one in sun, moon, star, or the translucent precious stone.

Facts frequently modify our human apprehensions of truth; there is Greek truth, Roman truth, and

Anglican truth, yet these are after all not *the* truth but modifications of the truth: truth is apprehended through the eyes of climates, educations, and traditions.

An old Hebrew begins to read his Scriptures, in an outward way, where the Christian leaves off. To the Christian the Hebrew begins at the end of his Bible to read through it; to the Hebrew the Christian does the same thing. The right way to the Hebrew is *his* way; the right way to the Christian is *his* way.

The savage man has one conception of beauty; the civilized man has another; each is right to each. When man was in a mere state of nature his god was a nature-god, a personification of natural forces.

When man began to inhabit houses, then he began to build temples for his God.

Man has always felt and said, that which is fitting for man is fitting for God.

The Homeric gods eat and drink, because, in the times of Homer, eating and drinking were divine pleasures. Zeus is the strongest of the gods, because strength was glorious and divine.

The ancient Germans were the most warlike people, so their supreme god was Odin the god of war. The Greeks and Romans came finally to deify accidents, passions, virtues.

Man's highest conception of himself is God. Man, however, feels his limitations; he projects himself into objectivity, and predicates of this objective self-infinitude the absence of all restrictions and limitations, and this is God. This is the best man can do — this is all he can do.

The Western nations have westernized Christianity: some believe to its betterment, some think to its detriment.

But of this transformation we cannot predicate right or wrong, better or worse, for religion must be not only in harmony with man's nature, but it must comport with zone and climate — with the rigid north or the genial south — with perpetual winter or perennial summer: with the dominance of the materialistic or the dominance of the spiritualistic. Christianity is universal, and yet the history of Christianity proves that wherever it has planted its foot it has been modified by the earth it touched. Some forms of life die when transplanted to uncongenial soils; some trees and flowers lose their identity by the new conditions of earth and moisture and temperature. The wide-leafed tree of the tropics — each leaf so full of the abundance of sunshine — huddles itself together to keep warm in our colder climate.

Religion, so self-adequate in the East, becomes organized in the West; that which is self-supporting in the one becomes mutually supporting in the other. Man becomes the measure of all things to himself.

A Brahmin knows the first half of the great commandment, and but little of the second. An Englishman knows the last half better than the first. A Brahmin can love God without loving his neighbour; an Englishman can love his neighbour without loving God.

The first, self-supporting, cannot enter into all

the organized forms of mutual helpfulness; the second, mutually supporting, cannot reach up to God without the love and help of his neighbour.

The Western mind makes sad havoc of the most spiritual sayings of Jesus. The beautiful words of the Master, "I and the Father are one," have been a strong proof-text of a physical, corporeal trinity. Put upon the plane of the material, it has got into the mathematical absurdity, that one thing is another thing — that Jesus meant to say that he was God and that God was himself; but once when a Christian missionary read these precious words to an old devoted Brahmin, he said, "Why, Jesus was a good Brahmin." He intuitively caught the spiritual import of the inspiring and encouraging words.

So, then, I conclude that truth is a term of metaphysics, and that right is a term of ethics.

In the abstract, there is but one true religion and many right religions; in the concrete, there is but one right religion and many true religions.

The truth of religion is the harmony between the

conception of the man and the reality of the fact; the right of religion is the agreement between the conception of the man and the conduct of his life; so that, whilst the truth of religion may be a subject of proper and profitable speculation, the right of religion demands conscientious endeavour and practice. The one is a matter of the intellect's pleasure, the other is a matter of the man's practice; the one has its seat in the reason, the other has its seat in the conscience. We have to do properly enough with both. We are morally accountable to God only for the last — the right of religion. A vital mistake at this point has been the foundation of all religious bigotry, exclusiveness, intolerance, and iniquities.

No one historic religion can claim to be the true religion; each may claim to be the right religion. He is the real atheist who denies love, justice, mercy, not he who denies that there is a God of love, justice, mercy. A man who believes in these believes in God, whether he will or not: he who denies these, though he assert faith in

God with all the vocabulary of the Creeds, is an atheist.

He is not an infidel, who does not *believe* in sympathy, denial, and vicariousness; but who in his life fails to *practise* them. He is a Christian who has faith in these, though he deny the person Christ; for to have faith *in* these, is to have the faith *of* Christ. A man may not know where the fruit grows which he eats, and the substance of which gives him sustenance and joy; but he knows his food who gives his strength to the God who nourished the fruit-tree, and to his brother who is also the offspring of God.

Then it concerns us particularly to inquire whether our religion be right rather than whether it be true. Indeed I am not prepared to say that in this world we shall ever arrive at a definition of true religion. Metaphysics is an expanding science; ethics an exacting one. The growth of intellect and its culture will probably take away from our speculations all of its so-called solid bases, and that which to our reasoning is true to-day may be false to-morrow. "Take away from the Greek the quality of being Greek, and you take away his existence." Just as involuntarily and necessarily as a Greek is a Greek, so involuntarily and necessarily his gods are Greek.

There was a time when Jupiter was as true to the Heathen, as Jesus is real to the Christian. He took no offence at the nature of Jupiter. It was *his* nature. "To every religion the gods of *other* religions are only notions concerning God, but its own conception of God is to it God Himself; the true God — such as He is in Himself."

The truth *in* religion is movable, the right *of* religion is stationary; what yesterday was true in religion to-day is sensualism; what is atheism to-day will be true in religion to-morrow. I do not affirm that we know no more of the truth of religion and in religion to-day than yesterday. I believe we shall know more to-morrow than to-day.

Things in religion were true once which are qualitatively untrue now. Many dogmas which were current coin half a century ago are counted spurious to-day. Indeed few of the views of religion prevalent then have any hold whatever upon the popular consciousness now, certainly none upon the culture and thinking of our time.

There is an antithesis between history and reason. Mankind was capable of receiving a statement of religion at one time which it is intellectually incapable of holding at another and an advanced time.

The Bible itself has the valuable merit of containing whatever the interpreter wishes to say. This is true of the scriptures of all religions, and it is most likely that it is this universal and indefinite element in the religious books of all nations that makes them Sacred Scriptures. Science had hard work to make the world believe that the form of the earth is spherical, because man in honesty supposed the Bible *revealed* its surface to be flat. Even theology now *compels* the Bible to be on good terms with the results of scientific inquiry.

In our youth we had no other idea of the processes and time of creation than that the whole was finished in six days; but now the veracity of the Bible is made to hold on its way, although we may be convinced that to bring the world to its present form and structure, may have required six million years.

The old theologians said, that the essential attributes of God were made manifest by the light of the natural reason, but the Trinity could only be known by revelation. This they had to say, because the theological Trinity contradicts the natural reason.

But, in reality when it is said an idea comes to us by revelation, it is simply meant it comes to us by tradition. The tradition of one age is the revelation of another.

The revelations of the Bible are as changeful, therefore, as human opinions and prejudices. And it is a wonderful book in this, that it throws illumination both ways, backwards and forwards. It is so universal in its spirit, its very language suits the thoughts of all ages.

But when we pass from the metaphysical speculations about truths of religion, to contemplate and consider the ethical duties of religion, we are left to no such doubts, dealings, and uncertainties.

Here we are compelled to allow each man to settle for himself the value of scriptures, revelations, traditions, sacraments, rites, and forms of worship. His religion is right whose religion rights itself with his own soul and God.

If a man be a Brahmin by the law of his conscience, he must be a Brahmin by the course of his conduct, if he would have the right religion, although Christianity may be a truer religion than Brahminism.

To be the votary of one sect in conscience, and of another by affiliation, involves a form of dishonesty and insincerity, detrimental to, if not destructive of, the highest, truest, sweetest, religious life.

Only that religion, furthermore, is right, which by its contents satisfies the subject of it, answers to his conscience, his ideals, his wants. It may be less true or more true than another, but if it consciously and well serves these ends, it is essentially right. A man knows when he is clothed and fed, though he may be ignorant of the texture of his garments and the constituents of his food.

Any religion which stretches out its helping hands, and says, "Come unto Me all ye that labor and are heavy laden, and I will give you rest," and fulfils to the heart the promise to the ear, is the right religion.

Being a law unto himself, one should be careful how he insists upon being a law to other people. We find the secret of life in the law of Jesus Christ, but each man must be left free to interpret this law for himself.

Happy he who finds in his own soul the rest of Christ's soul. He may come to this through cathedral ceremonials, or in the caverns of the earth. The Spirit of God has an easy way of finding men out and rising up like a great mountain to keep off the wintry blasts from their souls.

There is a rest at the very heart of the universe, which distils itself as morning dew upon the thirsty heart of humanity. It quickens in this soil, and the fruit is of the seed after its own kind and fashion. They who eat of this fruit find the promised rest.

Justice, mercy, humility, these are religion. Justice puts *us* on an equal footing with all. Mercy lifts the lowliest to an equal footing with ourselves. Humility teaches us there is no *condescension* in God, when He chooses man for a companion.

Religion, which is the avowal of the heart, *to itself*, of its re-allegiance to its God, is right when it tests its loyalty by patriotism to humanity.

THE SURE HELL

"In a valley, centuries ago,
Grew a little fern leaf, green and slender —
Veining delicate, and fibres tender —
Waving, when the wind crept down so low;
Rushes tall, and moss, and grass grew round it,
Playful sunbeams darted in and found it,
Drops of dew stole in, by night, and crowned it,
But no foot of man e'er trod that way;
Earth was young, and keeping holiday.

Monster fishes swam the silent main,
Stately forests waved their giant branches,
Mountains hurled their snowy avalanches,
Mammoth creatures stalked across the plain;
Nature revelled in grand mysteries,
But the little fern was not of these,
Did not number with the hills and trees;
Only grew and waved, its sweet wild way,
No one came to note it, day by day.

Earth, one time, put on a frolic mood,
Heaved the rocks, and changed the mighty motion
Of the deep, strong currents of the ocean,
Moved the plain, and shook the haughty wood,
Crushed the little fern in soft, moist clay,
Covered it, and hid it safe away;
Oh, the long, long centuries since that day!
Oh, the agony! Oh, life's bitter cost,
Since that useless little fern was lost!

Useless? Lost? There came a thoughtful man,
   Searching Nature's secrets, far and deep;
   From a fissure in a rocky steep
He withdrew a stone, o'er which there ran
   Fairy pencillings, a quaint design,
   Veinings, leafage, fibres clear and fine,
   And the fern's life lay in every line!
   So, I think, God hides some souls away,
   Sweetly to surprise us, the last day."

THERE is one point of agreement in all systems of religion; namely, that suffering is the sequence of sin. All wrong-doing does not bring pain and remorse, however; for the moral quality of an act takes its character sometimes from a century, sometimes from climate, sometimes from conventionalism; yet there is in all centuries, climates, conventionalisms — that is in all civilizations — a standard of ethics, a law of right and wrong. This law may be a supposed revelation from God, or the edict of some vicegerent of God, or the monition of the conscience. Each man possessed of the sanity of accountability has a law of morality; to live in accordance with its approvals is to live righteously, to be brought under the voice of its condemnations is to live sinfully.

The same act may have an unlike moral character to different minds, the result of dissimilar educations. Notwithstanding this, it is always and everywhere right to do right, and wrong to do wrong; so every volitional act refers itself to a standard which determines it to be right or wrong. The wrong act brings pain, the right act brings peace.

There is no relief to the transgressor in the persuasion that there are no abstract and absolute moral distinctions, or that these are only the yokes of kingcraft and priestcraft; for if morality is resolved into utilitarianism, then that is right which is best, which is only exchanging one ground for another, the *ought* of the conscience for the *ought* of the conventionalism.

Society must determine what is best for itself, and the individual must conform to its dictates. Although we may persuade ourselves that moral distinctions are not abstract and absolute, we cannot persuade ourselves that they are *unreal.* For morality is as real as the consciousness of God;

indeed, it is the creature of this belief in God. The two are identical in conception; when the mind refers itself to God, it refers itself to an ideal standard of morality. The need of the soul that brings God into it is the same that craves the approval and peace of God, and shuns his condemnation and displeasure. There is then no process by which the *reality* of the ethical idea can be abrogated and annulled. That philosophy which says, "Let us eat and drink, for to-morrow we die," counts eating and drinking its chief good, and *so* right: it accepts all the consequences of this course of life, as preferable to the consequences of an opposite course.

But even this philosophy does not hope to escape consequences. When man accepts one theory of life, and comports his conduct with another, morality is a law of bondage to him, it limits him, walls him in, and involves him in a web of entanglement; he breaks one chain to find he is bound by another; he is the subject of conscious spiritual anarchy, and he wears himself out in reproaches and remorses which take the sweetness out of all life's roses, and turn to bitterness on his tongue every delight. This man is unreconciled to himself. He begins the effort to get rid of the ideal standard, but this is now utterly impossible, for if it no longer reminds him, it never ceases to haunt him. It may be too indefinite to be called an image, but it is certainly real enough to be called a spectre. If it does not work conformity, or contrition, then condemnation. When we have found and affirmed the antithesis between the standard of the conscience and the rule of conduct, we have indicated the first element of the hell-idea. God is in harmony with himself; man to be like God must be in harmony not only with God, but with himself, in accordance with his circumstances and his nature. The free issue of his soul must be seen in free action; that is, his delight must be in the law of his own being. In looking upon the course of a beautiful river, it never occurs to us that the waters are offended and rebellious because it is their nature so ceaselessly to flow on and flow on ceaselessly in one path.

The exceeding glory of the river is that it is in harmony with its own nature and God's nature, and so completely in accord with its own impelling power and destiny.

The violet comes up, not repining that it came no sooner, or was not allowed to continue folded so warmly in the love of the earth, but feeds upon the sunshine and moisture as its appointed way of getting and giving life. The pious little flower rejoices in its own law, and so delights itself in the law of the Lord.

When man breaks this order of being, feels the inherent law of harmony at variance with the law of his own desires and appetites, — wills one way and acts another, — he separates himself from the universal law, is thrown off from his own harmony; the harmony of law and God, and so is in the outer darkness of rebellion and discord.

The impassable gulf, however, between heaven and hell is not the distance between purity and sin, but between penitence and impenitence.

Heaven is that estate of the man where purity is

loved and sin detested: hell is that condition of the soul where purity is detested, and sin is loved. The fact that the universal conscience approves of the right, and disapproves of the wrong, is the pledge of the normality of virtue; that purity is the natural condition of man, that man is best off, and only well off, when in spiritual accord with his own nature, — to know this, to feel this, until it begets serious strivings and earnest endeavours, is heaven; to know this, and feel this, and rebel against it, hate the right, revel in the impure, is hell.

Man, then, in the state of nature — I mean, of course, man when most natural, most like himself — most like, not this individual or that individual, but most like the ideal humanity — is in the state of grace nearest to God, most surrounded by heaven.

The last born infant, just from God, is the newest revelation from God, the new testament of his love and favour, the renewed testimony of his imminence.

The further removed from the centre and concord, the more conscious of a law of the flesh warring against the law of the Spirit. *To be content in the warfare is hell.* This is simply preferring spiritual chaos to spiritual cosmos, with no sighings and seekings for the conforming Spirit of God. No penitence or contrition because of the darkness which hides God from the spirit, no regret at the presence of the demon of discord — this is hell. Hell, then, is not that state of intellectual confusion which calls good evil, and evil good, but that state of moral obtuseness which loves evil rather than good, and darkness rather than light. The regret is not for the sin, but because of the law which makes it sin. The sorrow works toward God, not toward the man.

The sense of God's presence in the soul is not only heaven then, but it is also hell.

This presence man both seeks and shuns: when the sense of God is in the heart through the seeking, it is heaven; when there through the shunning, it is hell. There are images and memories which remain in the mind by the very effort of the mind to get rid of them. The mind knows, probably, no such torture as this. The man may not always be cognizant of God's presence, but the very fact of the effort to get rid of it demonstrates the consciousness of it. And God is not the obedient slave of man's will; He will not be drawn out of His own temple. Man may ruthlessly, with iconoclastic intent, break every symbol and image of the living God in his own heart, but the vestal lamp still burns so brightly that hidden sin is discovered, and the excellent glory of God is revealed. To behold sin in juxtaposition with God, to choose sin and refuse God, to love the deformity, and hate the perfection,—this is hell. When the demons of the soul cry out, "Thou Son of the living God, leave us alone," then hell has entered in and taken possession of the man.

Now, if it could be, if it were spiritually possible, for the soul to realize that this estate, self-chosen, could become normal and natural, that God would go out and stay out, and leave him to his own moral affinities and delights in this world or *in eternity*,—then the sinner would have gained his end, and the mastery over the laws of the moral universe and God. Then, for him, hell would be heaven. But this conception, so prevalent, is monstrously absurd. Hell is hell because in it there is an open way to heaven. Because God's Spirit is even there! — there to accuse of shame, and to entreat — there to renew offers of mercy, forgiveness, and saving help. Not to impose these, but to proffer them. Hell is where something better may be attained — where effort is possible. We have been taught to believe that hell is a refuge for the will-less, whereas such a refuge would be their heaven.

No, the constraining love of God gives the rebellious child no refuge from the torturing conscience, though he make his bed in hell. This is the "worm that dieth not, and the fire that is not quenched."

Hell is just that juncture, whether in time or in eternity, that confluence of certainty and realization, in this world or in the next, where the soul has settled it that it must repent, and yet hates the tears and sobbings of contrition. *Postponement is hell;* something must be done, yet the doing is deferred.

There is in this association of ideas one that contravenes the pompous dogmatism so prevalent in theologic speculation, namely, that hell is vindictive punishment; for it illumines the truth of spiritual sequence so unmistakably and grandly that God no longer is covered in hideous darkness, the righteousness of his moral government is no longer called into question when it is made so palpably plain, that only an unvindictive hell is, in reality, hell at all.

A vindictive hell is a fancied vision of vindictive priestcraft. The subject of such a hell would then be guiltless. He could no longer feel that he is the wrong-doer, but God is the wrong-doer. He may still have the recollection of his wrong-doings, but he only did in his lifetime what God is doing in eternity.

There can be nothing revengeful in God, or in nature, or in morals. These hell-spectres are only the phantoms of bad men's brains, and I am persuaded they are only the endeavours of men to get rid of the inevitable hell, which pursues and enfolds the wrong-doer until he consents to turn to God and live.

If the Scriptures of our religion should contain never so many separate and isolated passages, stating in the most unmistakable language that man is liable to endless punishment for his misconduct in this life, then I frankly confess the sincere and reverential believer would be morally bound to accept one of two alternatives: either to insist that these texts of the Scriptures must be interpreted to harmonize with the revelation of God's infinite love and man's original sense of justice, which would virtually be taking all meaning out of them; or, secondly, to deny unequivocally the truth of their statement, which would be nothing more than the reason of one man set up in candour and reverence against the opinion of other men.

If I am now told I do not believe in the Bible, I answer, the first tenet of my creed, as I learn it from all Bibles, is not "I believe in hell," but "I believe in God;" and hell must be explained by my faith in God, and not God explained by my faith in hell.

It is incredible that a man, both devout towards God and sincere towards himself, should even accept the possibility of man's continuing eternally a sinner, and in the hell of sin, or hold to the preposterous theory that eternity is, in the Divine economy, only a vindication of time.

The moral structure of the human mind makes it impossible to contemplate any such issue of life. To accept it is possible, to conceive it impossible. Men who do right because they fear to do wrong, fear not hell, but exposure; they acknowledge to themselves, not accountability to God, but to society. Man, indeed, cannot do right because he fears to do wrong, for in this attempt the quality of hypocrisy enters in to destroy absolutely all quality of virtue.

Nowhere in God's limitless space or infinite time is suffering the dreadful thing, but sinning. It is only the exceeding sinfulness of sin which is seen in suffering; suffering tells the tale of sinning.

It is horrible to believe that, for the sake of the suffering, the sinning is eternal!

No; the last soul must repent at last, and repent that he did not repent before.

One holy, helpful man said he lived upon the confines of hell to be near heaven.

This is the very heart of our philosophy—the highest heaven adjoins the deepest hell. He who toils amongst the lowest is himself the highest. He who has greatest faith in the most depraved has greatest faith in the most divine.

Dear God! how sweet heaven will be to Thee when all Thy children get home!

God will not for ever carry the pains and griefs that pierce and burden the hearts of his little ones. To this release He works with them, and for them, and in them; and this shall be an effectual working unto life. God's universe is His New Jerusalem, and its streets shall be searched until the last lost jewel is found. The Father knows the names of all His children, and when the feast of the First-born is celebrated, all shall have heard the call and come home.

VI

THE TRUE HEAVEN

I cannot think but God must know
About the thing I long for so;
I know He is so good, so kind,
I cannot think but He will find
Some way to help, some way to show
Me to the thing I long for so.

I stretch my hand — it lies so near;
It looks so sweet, it looks so dear.
"Dear Lord," I pray, "Oh, let me know
If it is wrong to want it so?"
He only smiles — He does not speak:
My heart grows weaker and more weak,
With looking at the thing so dear,
Which lies so far, and yet so near.

Now, Lord, I leave at thy loved feet
This thing which looks so near, so sweet;
I will not seek, I will not long —
I almost fear I have been wrong.
I'll go, and work the harder, Lord,
And wait till by some loud, clear word
Thou callest me to thy loved feet,
To take this thing so dear, so sweet.

Saxe Holm.

THAT which was personal to himself Jesus made universal to humanity. He saw the race in himself, rather than himself in the race. He became in himself the standard of humanity, not humanity the standard of himself. This is all the meaning there is in the miraculous birth of Christ. All men spiritually have been born into humanity, humanity spiritually was born into Christ.

He felt that humanity should be what he was, whereas all other men have felt they should strive for the ideal humanity.

He was, then, the realization of the desire of nations. This is miraculous in this, that it has occurred but once; not that it may not occur again, not that it is contrary to the laws of Nature and life that it should occur a thousand times in the future. For aught we know, this may be the truest and deepest law of God and Nature, and, because so profound, it has enacted itself, so far as we know, only once in the history of humanity.

When the time comes that this shall be the custom, and not the exception, this term miraculous will have lost its import, for this is all the meaning it has. Nature is one, and cannot be divided; we get one aspect of Nature in one century, another aspect in another century; but her essence cannot be two. She stretches out her hand in one century and creates man. She reveals her face in another to bless man.

Christ fulfilled in himself his own conception of himself, and it was this harmony of the ideal and actual that made him the revelation of God to man, and the revelation of man to God. He brought God and futurity into humanity and time: into our homes, workshops, and experiences. He affirmed the immortality of all men, upon the basis of the Spirit's affirmation of immortality in himself.

This became the essentiality of *his* life, which he referred to all lives. He made universal a consciousness which was personal to himself.

He *said* all men are immortal, because he *felt* he was immortal.

His affirmation, then, was based upon an assumption. He applied to all men that which he knew of himself. He affirmed of the genus humanity what he knew of the personal man. This man was the best and most perfect of the species, and it is the very genius of spiritual faith to affirm of all that which we can affirm of the highest type.

Personal immortality was fundamental to no ancient system of philosophy; among the heathen it had only the significance of a subjective conception, and this conception was vague, confused, and contradictory.

Plato unmistakably taught the immortality of the race — on this wise, and in these words: "The human race, then, is interlinked with all time, which follows and will follow it to the end, being in this way immortal; inasmuch as leaving children's children, and being one and the same by generation, it partakes of immortality."

It is foreign to my purpose to appreciate Jesus, by depreciating Plato, or to rest in the testimony of either, when reporting upon matters which pertain to Spirit and futurity. I simply quote the Greek as adding confirmation to the Hebrew. He believed what the other knew.

A landscape is the more beautiful that we have seen it in its two aspects, when in dimness and uncertainty, by the haziness about it; and when in full revelation that all mist is dispelled. Plato was the morning of faith, Jesus its noon-day. Immortality was the obvious inference of Christ's own consciousness. We believe in goodness by believing in men. Christ begets faith in purity, and to get very near to Christ is to make very clear immortality to the spirit's comprehension. For the consciousness of God in the soul is the pledge of heaven. That nature which responds to God is that which is peculiarly certain that it is unsuited to attain its highest development in this life. Through this, man is akin to God, and in this nature of man is lodged the assurance of immortality; in most men it may not assume the strength of demonstration, rather only a glimmer of futurity thrown back from God into the soul of his child, and strengthened as the child lays hold on it, and works with it and by it. The light of eternity lies in the heart; by it man sees a little way, if not far into the future. When this light becomes the soul's illumination, and through it the soul becomes translucent, *the future is now* and *now is the future.* The wall of partition is broken down, and there is no such thing as a distinction in time — none in immortality. *This* is eternity, *this* is heaven; eternity is all time, heaven is everywhere.

The Brahmin confuses two conceptions which the Christian keeps separate, the God-life and the immortal life — that the spirit, having emanated from God, never finds its equilibrium and poise, its content and rest, until restored back to God: not in the Christian sense of spiritual affiance, but the philosophic sense of spiritual identity, so that immortality becomes the essence of God, or rather God is immortality. Personal immortality is the endless maintenance of the personal identity. And we are instructed in this by the very *need* of it; without this friendship is a dream, and love a delusion.

A little grave is often heaven's open way to a mother's heart, and the spirit-life of her child is as real and unquestioned as was the earth-life. Once her heart was the home of the child. Now her child is the home of her heart. Distance — no; separation — no, not even that; but dimmed vision has not broken love, but cemented it, as the loss of one faculty sharpens another.

Friendships begin to grow here which must have eternity in which to mature.

Men begin to redeem themselves here, giving promise and pledge to themselves of something better than they have been; the tendrils of their souls begin to cling up to the invisible presence of God, turn from the dampness and darkness of sin to the warmth and sunshine of God. And fate shall not mock the very springs of this new life, but shall fulfil in the reality the promise to the heart. Man is immortal, because man believes it *best* he should be.

Nothing that has ever been said about heaven can greatly help man to faith in it.

This is the unfolding of man's own life — it flowers into immortality. By day and by night, by visions and by dreams, by joys and by sorrows, through all these by the unfolding of his own nature, his own immortality becomes an assurance to himself.

Man emphasizes eternity, just as eternity emphasizes man; he dwells in the future just as the future dwells in him. "He that loveth not God knoweth not God."

The logic and order are reversed; knowledge comes of love, not love of knowledge. Tears of penitence give sight of purity. The pure in heart see God. When there is struggle between intellect and feeling to gain this, he who keeps possession of the field wins. The demands of intellection, when they are exacting, surrender finally to the behests of aspiration; what the spirit sees, it sees with greater certainty and precision than the in tellect. Reason may *doubt* the report of the spirit, but must not deny, for in time the lagging critical faculty will see what the diviner and primal consciousness affirms.

There is no contradiction between music and language. It is the function of the one to express sentiment, of the other to express thought.

These frequently cross paths, and usurp each the other's calling and faculty; but language must not envy music, nor music envy language — we must accept the testimony of both. The purposes of language are the more ordinary, of music the more exceptional.

The intellect can say what it cannot sing, the spirit can sing what it cannot say. Whether is the diviner, the speech or the song, must probably depend upon the responsiveness of the listener, and "to him that hath shall be given." Most of us *feel* that the requiem has a higher meaning than the oration.

Speculation has deferred the reappearing of the Lord; indeed has transposed the very words of the Spirit, which are that *we* are to tarry for his coming again, into, he is to tarry for our appearing.

The vision of the New Jerusalem was not that of an ascending city, but a descending city. The voice out of heaven said, "Behold, the tabernacle of God is with men, and He will dwell with them."

The apocalypse closes with heaven upon earth, not earth transported to heaven. The holy city, clothed with the glory of God, is descending in answer to the universal prayer men have been offering up all these ages, mistaking its words and knowing not its answer, "Thy kingdom come, Thy will be done on earth."

Heaven is not locality, except that every point of space is heaven, where God's will is the law of life.

Everywhere in the universe, a willing child in the arms of the loving Father is heaven. And where else can the child find rest?

The securities of Church and sacrament are worthless. The idle vagaries of psalm-singing and star-gazing around the throne of God are delusions; — nursery tales suited to the imaginations of children, and the superstitions of credulity.

Heaven, as a place of aimless idleness and intolerable vanity, accepted as a reward and held as a bounty, happy in the sense of escape while gazing into a hell of misery — is the device of the same bigotry which has not learned that respectable selfishness is worse than ignorant indulgence.

The redeemed spirit could find no heaven whilst a brother spirit was in hell, save the heaven which would fill and glorify his soul in the endeavour to rescue the wanderer.

He who would enter such a theologic heaven as these conspirators against humanity have surveyed, and to which only they themselves have the deed, is himself far from the Kingdom. He has broken faith with the Mystic Brotherhood. The signet of the Divine Knighthood is sacrifice. Its chivalry would bear it to the gates of hell, and there demand admittance to rescue a comrade. Heaven cannot be satisfied till hell has surrendered up its last lost child. He who seeks heaven may find it. Every childless mother who hears the cough of a motherless child and takes its sickness upon her own heart, and presses her heart against the little cough until it is gone, as if by magic, has entered in and *is* at rest. The man who teaches the ragged class in Sunday School only once, and sees they are clothed and warmed for the next time, has entered the open way to life. The heart of God is the universal heart of humanity; get near to one, and we get near to the other. The only angels of which we know any thing are the angels of living children. "Take heed that ye despise not one of these little ones; for I say unto you, that in heaven their angels do always behold the face of my Father which is in heaven."

How near we are to heaven in the faith that heaven is so near to us!

The odours of the orange-grove are wafted to us before we enter it. We cannot mistake the proximity of heaven, the air is so heavenly.

And the volume of the Book of Life shall have

no seal upon it — all may know that the names of all are written therein.

The gates of the descending city shall not be shut at all — open until the last and farthest away has come in.

And then not shut; even the sign of exclusion shall not be about it.

www.ingramcontent.com/pod-product-compliance
Lightning Source LLC
LaVergne TN
LVHW021413110826
845150LV00007B/1906

* 9 7 8 1 4 2 5 5 1 0 5 8 9 *